CONSTANTLY SINGING

'An' constantly singin', no less, when he ought always
to be on his knees offerin' up a Novena for a job.'

Mrs Boyle in Sean O'Casey's *Juno and the Paycock*

'Anything processed by memory is fiction!'
Wright Morris

Dedication
for Imelda

There were no poems that year,
but every night driving from work
the red haws on the hedges
took me unawares, looming
in the milky car beams
as lush as cherries;
a sign they said of the hard
winter to come or maybe
the loveliest summer
in living memory,
my memory, my dear.

CONSTANTLY SINGING

James Simmons

Blackstaff Press

ACKNOWLEDGEMENTS

Some of these poems have appeared in *Aquarius, Chapman, Cyphers, Dublin Festival Anthology, Gown, The Honest Ulsterman, The Irish Press, The Irish Times, Madog, New Leaf, New Poems 77-78, P.M.3, Quarto, A Sense of Ireland: The Writers, The Stoneferry Review, Words*, or have been broadcast by the BBC.

Published by Blackstaff Press Limited, 3 Galway Park, Dundonald, Belfast, BT16 0AN, with the assistance of the Arts Council of Northern Ireland.

ISBN 0 85640 217 6

Printed in Northern Ireland by W & G Baird Ltd.

Contents

Meditations in Time of Divorce
for Michael Foley

Society Street: 1977

1

The economics of marriage:

when alimony splits the salary
you're poor again, like a student
at forty-five, staring out
of your rented terrace house
at the grey pebble-dashed wall
of the Presbyterian Hall
always in shadow.
               All he can know
of sunset is the red bricks
of houses across the street,
when they glow.

2

Like a poor student. Yes,
drunk with possibilities.

A Protestant, a Pilgrim,
seedy environments suit him.

Ancient Ireland's monks and sages
had small houses, hermitages,

for the soul's dark night, for mystic trances,
not keeping up appearances.

In dowdy narrowness, not gloom
but music fills the sitting room.

Call sitting room and hall and yard
workshop and shelter for the bard.

The diner, recently the cook,
washes the dishes, opens the good book.

3

Courage and rigour
obviate simony,
pursuing the wild game
through thickets of irony.

The free agent breaks moulds
and casts out remorse.
The sign and test of it is
old chores are blessed.

Behold the change-shaper,
now Ulster's leading
lighter of a fire
with screwed up newspaper,

a dish-washer of genius — see,
entranced over the cracked sink,
his hot water and Fairy Liquid
slide grease from cutlery.

Wife memory devises,
in table wiping and draping
dishcloths over taps to dry,
new spiritual exercises.

He is tempted to God-pose.
He intones, 'Life is good!'
and the best disciple's response
is to snigger, 'Platitudinous old pseud.'

2

4

With twenty dedicated years
of collected tape-recordings
his mean shelves are crammed.
They have him by the ears.

Trivial rounds and common tasks
embellished and glorified
by immortal voices, taped 78s
of The Weavers and John McCormick, are all he could ask.

Gene Kelly singing, 'Love is here to stay,'
and Bessie, 'Gimme a pig's foot.'
Finney reading D. H. Lawrence
in Nottinghamese, Third Programme plays.

Devlin and Mary Farrell in *All that Fall*,
Pinter's mandarin tribute
to 'Mac', Scofield as Lear.
How right he was to record them all!

This is his church. Rising from our dirt
we cross ourselves, crossing the street.
The aisle is full of strange noises
that give delight and do no hurt.

5

A metallic siren wakes him now
for work, as the wife used to.
Unhelped, unhampered by once-loved
facilities, he rises on will-power
and takes in the emptiness
that surrounds him, the narrowness,
the strange proximity
of mass-produced metal windows.

Lacking curtains so far
he must content himself to see
the wrecked backyards. It used to be
broad skies over the Atlantic,
white wooden bathing houses
on the bent wall of the harbour, a great
crescent of sand, gull cries.

Nevertheless he feels potential
not loss. Like Saint Patrick he rises
reciting, up to his neck in cold
comfort, in good faith embracing
necessity, constantly singing, not
putting a sour face on it.

Alas for her the change is deprivation,
hence acrimony and divorce,
seizing the house-beautiful, the car,
the kids, lacking other resource.

6

On the rocks he has to flower,
a sort of back-street merman
singing weirdly of a landlocked family,
left and remembered painfully.

He never enjoyed luxury; but, oh,
rearing a family, however unnatural,
was sweet: the dwarf night garments
by the fire, scented with talc,
children's daft creative abuse
of language . . .

Penelope swooned
towards her father, offering all herself
outstretched to be carried, crying,
'Lakalady, lakalady!' and, hoisted up
on his shoulders, rode more like a lady
than any he ever knowed . . .

Conducting now from a distance
his cheques and good wishes fly in the post,
he is glimpsed occasionally, a ghost
at outings and once-off celebrations,
a presence beyond the television's glow;

but ruefully invigorated,
at home at sea, hated only
out of grief, loved, lost,
looked for from the big windows
occasionally.

7

I will never go back.
They will not come to me;
but laughter, worried expressions
and quirks of personality

like voices on the wind
penetrate occasionally
to my soul and scar me.
That I must seem unkind.

Twenty years is a long time to play
at marriage; but all my gardens
went to seed, all our houses
decayed in my tenancy.

8

Coleraine center,
the Latin Quarter
imagined by Ulster lads
of the Fifties,
where Henry Miller,
the master of cliché,
Fitzgerald and Hemingway
were young writers in love with a city
that left them free,
living cheaply, accepted,
their Olivetti portables
on worn tables at window shrines,
white paper our only luxury
marked by prose sentences

as fresh as the croissants
and unwrapped vegetables
our girls carried graciously
singing up the stairs.

If youth is wasted on the young,
wisdom is wasted on the middle-aged
if we don't have the wit to do now
what we always wanted.

9

He discovered an almost rural way
to walk to work yesterday
across the cemetery.
His father is buried here
and he loiters looking down
on a small desolate empty
arena with black marble walls.

Instead of meditating on death
he finds something to do, kneeling
clearing a few square feet of weeds,
secure in dreams of a good
future that will come true.

Today, taking the same way
to work, there are plants on a wooden bench
for sale outside a shop.

He arrives at the grave
with a brown parcel spilling clay.
Fingers, not often calloused
by spade work, poke holes
for the frail roots of flowers
and press the earth home gently.

All smiles, in solitude, constantly singing
he can relish the graveyard tap running
the black clay off his hands coldly.

Dirty fingernails all that day
will remind him. At desk and at lectern
two gesturing hands will convey
a personal message: 'I have knelt to honour
my father's grave, the ashes of my ancestor.'

On Sunday he brings his mother who smiles to see
her prodigal son rejoining the family.

10

Surprised by joy —
to make this day complete
at midnight he hears knocking,
his girl walks out of the street

unexpected,
a half bottle of Powers
in her shoulder bag.
They sit till all hours.

Her only jazz musicians
have been Mingus and Coltrane.
When he plays her *West End Blues*
She asks to hear it again.

They drink the pure gold whisky
and listen and talk.
It seems there is nothing they try for
that doesn't work.

She has a good job and enjoys it
so they set the alarm
and drift to sleep in silence
her head on his arm.

One night they were still kissing
when the dawn broke
on the ruined backyards,
a lugubrious joke

it seemed, in their joy,
Victorian spectres
of poverty, to scare THEM —
the board of directors!

Eden

He threw them out and slammed the gate shut
for what He found them up to. He was scared
like all angry people and unprepared
for love. He decided to blame it on 'that slut'.

Morally hung over He walked the walls,
straightened His stone picnic-tables, stared
sickly at the new padlock and the guard's sword,
waiting to welcome repentant prodigals.

If only they'd argue, face to face; but no.
They sneaked back to pick up a radio
left in a secret place in the undergrowth,
aimlessness their element they were loath
to risk losing. They drifted into the night,
relieved in every way to travel light.
The unprejudiced world was what those two lacked,
and of course they avoided the huge pathetic back
of God. To this day He is standing there,
banished. There *was* a world elsewhere.

After Eden

His last glimpse of the former wife
is after midnight, woozy with drink,
on a quick foray for old tapes,
and the front door is open, as always,
out of their shared instinct.

A ghost in his own shadowy hall,
the stairwell echoing still
with bitter shouting and slammed doors,
up in his old study he opens drawers,
and descends, his thieving arms full.

A man comes out of the kitchen and disappears.
At the car the wife grabs him, hissing abuse.
Hunched awkwardly, unloading his loot,
his high-pitched voice whining, 'Christ
you've got everything else!' — he breaks loose,

'Look! We agreed . . .' 'I agreed to nothing!
It was YOU walked out on ME with your whore!'
When he hits her, precious tapes unreel
and roll on the pavement. Again they are sharing
intimate touch — her nose, his knuckles, sore.

Will the long marriage never be over?
Love she would call what drives her now to close
fiercely against him, drinking his anger,
shameless and righteous, fronting
her husband, embracing his futile blows.

His last glimpse is of her standing
in faded chiffon nightwear, humble, beautiful,
like a dark harvest etching, The Last Gleaner,
a woman, lit by a street lamp, winding
tangles of gleaming tape on a plastic spool.

The Baggage and the Toff

Her long straight uncombed tangled tresses
and miscellaneous modern dresses
and double chin and sloppy carriage
led to her being called a baggage,
while he was an outstanding figure
somewhat declined in shape and vigour
but proud. The Baggage and the Toff:
these two were star turns, nothing put them off.

He muttered, 'Mutton dressed as lamb
when all is said is what I am
in this mod gear, these ear rings.'
'Better than shapeless cardigans
and pointy shoes,' she answered back,
brave as a lion, sharp as a tack.
This lovely Baggage and her Toff
were star turns, nothing put them off.

'Pathetic, Ireland's laughing stock,
stinkers,' the Toff's wife used to mock;
but she was lonely, and the hurt
seek consolation throwing dirt.
He heard her grief and felt more sick
at each pathetic dirty trick.
These two, the Baggage and her Toff,
were star turns, nothing put them off.

Wrapped in themselves they travelled far,
slugging dry sherry in the car.
Well after midnight, tired, to come
to someone else's holiday home
too early in the year, too short
of time and money, in good heart!
These two, the Baggage and the Toff,
were star turns, nothing put them off.

In clammy darkness they undressed
and bedded down on a mattress
with hairy blankets and damp sheets,
and then performed endearing feats
of love, in spite of haunting guilt
towards wife and children that he felt;
these two, the Baggage and the Toff,
were star turns, nothing put them off.

The Toff was long and fairly thin,
it seemed she was in love with him.
She lit a candle, just to go on
looking, and let it burn till dawn.
He woke and could not sleep again,
his bloodstream filled with caffeine.
These two, the Baggage and the Toff,
were star turns, nothing put them off.

Her beauty, everyone could see,
expressed a moral quality
hard to put words on; but he tried
often, until they split their sides
at each new cliché-ridden effort
that undigested passion offered.
These two, the Baggage and the Toff,
were star turns, nothing put them off.

By morning they were pleased to see
beyond the glass an alder tree.
Its mottled, crinkled leaves were moving
gently, a shrine beside the loving
who moved in almost silence over
from one embrace into another
gently as the sunlight moved
among the leaves the wind moved.

He said her skin was Arctic furs
on that firm skeleton of hers.
He touched with an exploring touch
as though his hands could tell him much.
She laughed. He stared, as if to see
the essence of her mystery.
These two, the Baggage and the Toff,
were star turns, nothing put them off.

The Honeymoon

Remember last summer when God turned on the heat
and browned our bodies, remember how hard and sweet
were the green apples you bought.
Remember how quickly neglected nipples were taught
to take pleasure in kissing. Remember your sunburn peeled
after a day on the grass of the hill field
and the painless scars evoked a principle for us,
that the truly lovely is truly ridiculous.

A beauty like you can look sometimes dumpy and fat,
knock-kneed, hen-toed, and none the worse for that,
for when you recover your splendour suddenly
what seemed like flaws is personality.
The world has examined you closely and found you right
and beautiful with a more piercing sight
than fashion editors know. You thought I meant
evasion, a left-handed compliment;
but now know better, being able to talk to you
like this is love being true.

Nothing could get us down those days together
but lust, on grass, in mountain streams when the weather
was hot as ourselves, on collapsing sofas, on floors,
in the steamed-up Datsun in the great outdoors.
Our best man swore you would be black and blue,
and, true enough, love's frightening. You do
violent seeming things; but no one's hurt,
playing by the rules. We rise from dirt,
stink, struggle, shining, having suffered nothing.
No wonder they say that God would have us loving.

The worst debâcle was, once, trying to screw,
erect, me knees-bent, on my feet, and you
tip-toe on Dickens's *Our Mutual Friend.*
No joy. Abashed, we thought it was the end
of something; but no, failing is all right,
a sort of roughage to the appetite.

Our strangest luck seemed, first, not good, but ill —
me slow to come, you inexhaustible.
That turned out well. I had not thought God's voice
was intricate and humorous, like Joyce's.

Even your tears, after our first quarrel
when you got strangely thick and I got moral,
were not exploitive. Remember our briny kiss?
Nothing was broken, nothing was amiss.

The Conservative

for Brian Friel

1

Time now to consider knickers,
frail gaudy triangles stretched
rich-textured as rope
in close-up on soft alps,
your alabaster bum.
                        Ah!
but your smile hardens.

                I am wrong,
I admit. Apparently gladrags
are not intended to tempt me
but to keep you warm. I laugh
but I'm not mocking!
                        Use
your historical imagination.

In my day, my other days,
suspenders, stockings, slips, etcetera,
were paradisal accoutrements
to be gained, regained.

Holding my mother's hand
in a shop in Ferryquay Street
where she bought thread, my glazed
eyes caressed the glossy card
on the counter, the Kayser Bondar girl
whose impossibly long dark legs
receded into clouds of underclothes
and a hard struggled in my schoolboy
shorts for recognition.

                        Go easy, love,
on a reformed old sexist, his agonies
of withdrawal, the long effort. Imagine
for instance one of those spruce and hollow
ex-alcoholics waking one morning

16

alone in a well-stocked bar who once
had begged and forced entry in the old
days of fierce addiction. To find it
all free and available and not to be touched!

'No, never touch it, thank you.' Oh,
the injustice! If only
I'd had you in my prime.

2

I am willing to learn, love,
but you must be able
to tell the intrinsic
from the fashionable.
It was no chauvinist
but a connoisseur
sighed as your bra hit the floor
carelessly, and your knickers
were off in a sweep inside your jeans.
You were wrong to cheat your lover
of such sweet scenes.

If this is freedom,
to fuck and be fucked
in puritan simplicity,
I am a counter-revolutionary.

Christians, who eat their god,
even, find It repetitive
lacking music and ritual.
Call me conservative —
but imagination and style
matter. You offer yourself — wow! —
and I will kneel and devour
my darling; but it matters how.

3

And this can be only beginning.

Under my banner will throng together
the rhyming poets and audible singers,
drummers with cymbal and brush, and bands
you can hear yourself talk above!

When the female string trios
arise from behind their potted
ferns the future is mine!

Oh, join me in that ecstacy
and I'll instruct you personally
in slow-foxtrots, in holding hands,
in sitting on knees. What could you want
more? . . . ordering cakes and teas
at Forster's Family Restaurant
where old-style waitresses in black
will teeter forward and teeter back
with the heavy silver service,
armoured in starched aprons
and unfailing servility.

Back. Back.
Let us follow my longings
to a Donegal again thronging
with faithful maids, and nannies
as sensual and superstitious
as John Hewitt's or Forrest Reid's
or Louis MacNeice's.

Remember that awful telephone call
ending an era, when Mrs Boal
stiffened, hoping she was mistaken,
and a faint voice from St Johnstown repeated
(with obviously drink taken),
'There are no maids left in Donegal.'

4

When your old conservative dies
keep your blue eyes dry.

Imagine me busy as usual
maybe in limbo, gathering
lost babies who died for causes
long forgotten since,
aborted by hot baths and gin
in sordid lodgings, aborted
in modern clinics under control,
hygienically done in.

The true conservative regrets
all loss, even dispersed semen
your soft mouth swallowed or spat
out, that I glimpsed smeared
on our glowing bellies, heaving
in ecstacy, being rubbed away,
evaporating, or trapped
in those feather light bags
we knotted so cheerfully
that lay all night at the bedside.

I remember hating thinking
of the fate of those half-hearted
waifs that descended monthly
for adoption out of oblivion,
that kept the faith. To this day
I sense them waiting while we
make pleasure, fading away.

5

If drop-out students
could drop in, then,
if forsaken girls and former
wives could be only

embraced again and explained to,
then usefully I could
wait out that interim,
as I wait for you now,
to hear your laugh, unladylike
behind me, the clink
of the half-bottle of whisky
or other strong drink,
your astounding cool arms
again interrupting my work,
your hair surrounding me.

But maybe it's not on.
Particular beauties may have to go
along with our bad habits.
The Provos may not know
themselves from the Stickies,
if in eternity no one bickers
over old hurtful distinctions,
if nothing that mattered matters
and nobody wears knickers.

Dunlewey: 1977

1

Somebody's summer house
out of season. Late at night
they arrived, unlocked it
and groped upstairs.

Quiet, tired, cold
they lay on an old mattress
at floor level by a low
window. Beyond in the wind

blackness was running wild,
the invisible pane of glass
shining faintly. No
sign of what they would see

in the morning: brightness,
a tapestry of leaves,
the upper branches
of an alder tree.

2

Rough blankets housed
the tender adulterers'
white delighted limbs,
their lovely groans and sighs.

Falling apart exhausted
they slept on their sides.
He dreamed his daughter, Helen,
was lost in a dark street

near home, but home was nowhere.
When fear released him
his opened eyes could see
a window full of stained leaves

and jointed alder branches:
when the leaves shook,
pieces of blue sky,
brown mountains.

3

Later they tidied the house,
turned electricity on
at the mains, lit fires
and followed the black plastic pipes

that led from the cistern
upstream to a waterfall.
They had joy in cooking
and joy in the gramophone.

But that was later,
after the dry Asalto and leisurely
fags, and Lester Young
playing *This Year's Kisses*.

The cover notes on the L.P.
had a wonderfully solemn tone.
'Vic Dickenson is a bucolic
Hamlet on the trombone.'

4

Maybe a wife was crying
far away; but news of the world
only came from the other window,
boys stirring, cars arriving

for Mass. Through lunchtime
rough voices rose in the bar
over the road. It seemed
they had not gone far enough . . .

but then her eyes absorbed him.
They watched a universe
of light domesticated
in small faults on the wallpaper.

They became aware
of a pale sun walking
gently around the house.
They just lay there.

5

They arrived almost too late
on the run from insoluble
complications; but lay down
in darkness, able to wait

for whatever the morning
would bring, the house to be all
they were hoping for,
and the lakes, and Errigal.

His watch strapped to his wrist
as he slept. 'What next?
When do we start?' he was asking,
turned on like a light switch.

No. He was there already,
the window before him, a leafy shrine,
to sunlight and love maybe,
and all her warmth behind him.

Cloncha

1

On their first quest
they followed an impulse of hers
thirty miles North and West
in search of an ancient cairn
some other boyfriend
had shown her, shared
with her.
         Relentless
she was with details,
tactless and true.
And yet he smiled,
learning and liking, and said
securely, 'I love you.'

'Stop! This is it.'
He stopped the car. 'No.'

He reversed six times
or more up narrow lanes,
harried by neck strain.

At last they asked a woman
who pointed over fields
to three high crosses,
standing (also patiently),
heavy with lost authority,
worn smooth, shapely,
landowners once in Ulster,
speechless now, gracefully
letting themselves be stroked.

2

Exploring delightedly
as lovers do
(shoddy their workmanship
as it is in all
of God's creatures)
they congratulated each other
on the view.

Sunlight and wind that day
brimmed the broad plateau
of Inishowen with air
like tinted water, submerging
every colour but yellow.

In petal and bloom of benweed
gorse and dandelion
bright yellow intensified.

White mist blurred
the edges of stone outcrops,
branches of willows,
sycamores, thorn hedges.

3

Modern poets and business families
live for their holidays —
Longley in Mayo, half
literary Ulster in Ardara.
Our hero's Arcady was here
with the bleak moors and strands,
for forty years near enough,
the Derry hinterland
between Foyle and Swilly
from Malin to Buncrana
to Greencastle to Shrove
Moville and Carndonagh.

The Anglo-Irish boy adores
broken demesne walls
empty condemned cottages
moorlands littered with boulders
gold-braided thinly with lichen,
sheeps' wool coarse and grey
from Lear's theatrical beard
on the rusted barbed wire,
the dried-blood red of rust,
the fragile brilliance of fuchsia
dancing dolls, a Japanese theatre
in country hedges grown native
and deserted like Yeats's plays,
pale water agile on slatey beds
of mountain streams, rain
on hotel windows, the pale gold
of whiskies set on the wine-dark
wood of country bar counters.

Today he searched for anecdotes
to establish his rights there,
retailed his mother's world of Moores,
Montgomerys, The Royal School,
Raphoe where young Magillicuddy of the Reeks
boarded, the names of her father's
two friends, Peter Sauce and Dorby Toye,
the aunts from Manorcunningham
who wouldn't inherit
a moneyless Scottish title,
Cunninghams, Rentouls, Kings, Craigs . . .
Nothing of this was his or him.

All he could offer honestly
was a private childhood, secrecy,
a boy drifting alone through fern
forests and alder groves, smoking
his first woodbine above Carrig Cnoc,

a consciousness apart from ancestors
and local inhabitants, a stranger
at home in the present moment
happily, then as now. He was luring
a girl near his heart in this
occupied country of his. His voice
touching another, the singer's art.

4

Truthfully he was ashamed
to be so much older,
too gratefully holding
beauty and youth.

Happy noises were going to be hollow,
however lovely she was,
if he wouldn't hear clearly
when the talk was callow.

But the feeling was there.
And what he learnt was this,
that what they felt was made
by what they were.

The value of love makes lovers
easy to scare.
In fear of loss, in fear
of opinions of others

they lift weapons of jealousy;
bribe, bargain, threat.
Hard to accept time alters.

It has not altered yet.

5

You've seen girls in the newsreels
running out of ruins
in ecstacy to embrace
an army of liberation.

A good moment in war.
The crazy celebrations
tell you how bad things were.

He didn't care who
set him free. He couldn't
do it himself, deadlocked
in bleak resistence,
hopelessly intimate
with his enemy.

Of course the girls step off
eventually. The battered
soldiers roar away.
In the free town
people may turn ugly.

There's not much that divides
armies objectively;
but you'd have to be very doctrinaire
not to fling your cap in the air
on days of liberation.

Peace grows out of war
grotesquely. Remember Stalin
the liberator and Eisenhower.

But Auschwitz is out of business,
Paris, though expensive, is free.

In private affairs
is less brutality.

6

Well, this was one more lover's quest,
lovely, neither first nor best.

They had to question whether
their love could last forever.

Contentment always says
something like promises.

The years from war to war
must be worth living for.

I sing of natural forces,
marriages, divorces.

Coleraine: 1977
for Desmond Maxwell

1

Hoping only for the best
and only hoping, here we are,
middle-class magi with no star
in the heavens or on our chests,
heading for country halls
with cultural promotions
and, afterwards, the bar
to enthuse or to drown
our sorrows after another let-down.

Just friends tonight sharing
the preparation of food and drink
the smell of beef cooking in blood
oil and onions, a bay leaf
floating in the casserole, aperitifs,
pictures, records, books . . .

we all have a certain flair
for enjoying each other
in a mildly bohemian fashion
and for lay acts of worship,
silent to hear
Bach's *St Matthew's Passion,*
vine leaves in our hair.

In the air, in our ears
in this narrow room is a power
and beauty none of us hopes to exceed,
artists and art's servants
that we are, bowing our heads
while the master work expands
to its full stature as it should.

Together, gladly enthralled, we savour
freedom in servitude. The future
is ours to work for, and, yes,
we believe in our creed;
but we have to ask ourselves,
is Bach what the people need?

30

2

At eleven o'clock
an explosion halts everything.
Stiff with shock, altered
involuntary, how can we take stock
of such an intrusion?

Out of curiosity then,
quick, cautious,
we sidle into the night air
like the rest of Coleraine,
fringing the street,
staring in the summer night.

A plain-clothes cop
has crashed, single-handed
out of the local boozer,
explosive with fear and hate,
grief for dead comrades,
to face nothing commensurate.

Now he is crouching behind his stretched
arms, stiff and twitching, his soft
finger hooked on a steel trigger.
We follow his tense aim across the street
to a straggle of hairy students.

Laden with carry-outs, reified,
languid with fear, geared
to a fashionable hatred of police,
they cower
by huge concrete vases
that form a barrier.
Inside the vases, in soil,
by civil edict
geraniums flower.

3

'Hold it! Hold it!' His voice
is desperately imitating
authority. Only killing
could ease this policeman;
but these are not his enemies.
They are not his people
at all, they are ours.

His eyes sweep the horizon
for Red Indians, by now drinking tea
in shabby housing estates, invisible,
watching themselves on TV,
preparing to strike again
quiet settlements like Coleraine.

Abandoned by craven citizens,
this is our only law-hero,
facing chaos alone, strong in a way,
willing to cross borders and bend laws
in a good cause, like Bach.

You might define decadence
by our ambivalence, unable to see or hear
exactly what's going on, only
the old words and music, our eyes
and ears curiously impaired.
Shops, churches, uniforms look
as they used to, but don't fill
the role. The rare policeman
with wit and integrity
is a poignant figure, like the clergyman
who embodies faith, or the rigorous teacher.

4

In Kingsgate Street window glass
is scattered in a familiar shop,
splinters scattered through the fruit
and vegetables. Sheer noise
distracted us, a showy trick,
melodramatic politics.

Bullied again, we have leant over
backwards to hear nothing.

5

At midnight, home again,
the delicate touch
of educated hands adjusts
volume and tone on hand-crafted
machinery that carries
the old music.
        A fiddle soars
under control over the busy
harpsichord. The great choir
is mounting the temple steps
of sound. Minds expand
in sympathy and awe, we three
worshipping, tippling whisky.

6

When Bach was on earth personally,
hiving away magnificently,
what violence broke his concentration?
What does his music say
about injustice and poverty?

Dark passages
uplifted into harmony.

7

At five a.m. Kingsgate Street
has gone back to the Indians.
Gulls, blackbirds whirr in wild
air between ghostly shops and houses.

Yesterday's papers float
and flop in the white light
of summer. The bomb went off
five hours ago. Alive
in our own excitement we explore
as far as Woolworth's and beyond.
The sky's wilderness descends
into the street where gulls whirr
and old newspapers stir.

A public clock strikes and the air
lightens again and the town hall
confronts us like an ancestor,
as cleanly built and etched clear
in the night air as the old prints
of this market town when the work ethic
had life more abundant.

You can set this down:
our work is not finished,
we are not terrified,
we walk abroad at all hours
in our home town.

8

Far away in America
I see, in imagination's light,
acres of desert, a reservation
that houses the stubborn remnants
of those original inhabitants
who stuff feather war bonnets
in the glove compartments of their Chevrolets
and ponder legal documents
on oil and mineral rights.

9

Tired out at six a.m.,
walking in profile,
between a past we can value
and the dumb explosions, the enveloping
smoke of activist politics
of those who don't turn up
at our promotions,

not powerful, not ridiculous,
we work on and wait
where desperation and hate
thrive and move the desperate.

Easter: 1950

The phone rings from London
dictating the market index in code.
Pen strokes in heavy ledgers record
oil shares owned and steel and gold.

This is his father's living, working
the world; but it's not real
to the young poet like the book in his pocket.
He has not learnt how to feel

the common energy of action
and transaction by which people rent
homes, get food and clothing.
He is living for something different.

Touchy, uncertain, a specialist
without qualifications, badly trained
in a boarding school where girls
were out of bounds and Ulster was England,

he will only do moronic tasks for his own
integrity. He sits for a year filing slips
of rough paper, dense with statistics
reduced from springs, cisterns, supply-pipes, drips.

The blank side of the cards appeals to him.
He doesn't know how often he follows his feet
down the back corridors, where old letters
and ledgers gather dust, to his toilet retreat.

On white spaces his pen burns theories
of pain, sensitivity and death, the case
against God, his only conversation.
The uncreated conscience of his race

is again being forged, clouded with melancholy:
'Oh, solitary yellow rose in the cold garden,'
he writes and sighs, and bites the apple to the core
of good and evil, assuming the burden

of discrimination. When his fellow clerk shouts
he pulls the ramshackle chain. Politely he will go
when his earthly father calls him, and yet
the one thing certain is he is saying No

to his father, uncomprehendingly,
like sulking, like stubbornness. Security
he will shrug off, as naturally as a bird
in autumn, and fly into obscurity.

The Poet's Father

His father is all tact. He seldom appears
in his own office and never interferes.
Once, in a long letter, he tried to explain
his interest in work, off-hand
philanthropy, good fun . . . in vain, he got a lecture
on the crimes of commerce from his son.

The father is living with a younger woman
thirty miles away, driving over in a draughty
van every day, a scandal in Derry.
The love they share, the good fun there
is drowning slowly in insults and snubs.
The pain they have left is hard to rise above.

'How can you think of your own selfish pleasures
when your wife is pining on her own?'
The father melts with tenderness for his son's
noble sentiments, his pompous tone.
In the silence between them he puffs his cigarette
ruefully in a world the poet has not entered yet.

He will take what's coming to him without
trying to explain. And he takes pleasure
less and less, aware of his wife's joyless
days, the incomprehension of friends
who have barred him from the club. A sociable man
in his fifties finds novelty and discomfort
hard to bear. A love-nest needs more effort
than the office. This Indian summer
of sexual pleasure makes him aware
of his worn body. There is thunder in the air.

When depression clouds the bright face
of his girl he begins fretting, guilty
shadows pass over his mind. When she dies
by her own hand, his impulse of relief
seems so contemptible he is never himself
again. Although his wife stays true
and kind, it seems booze and cronies is all
he can live up to. He opts out,
having too much to assimilate
of what his son is going to write about.

At the Post Office

1

He stumbled out of school, a hearty aesthete,
middling scholar and failed athlete,
the third best poet, maybe,
at Campbell College, shining still
with all the garments of potential,
a cigarette in a Rupert Brooke profile.

That last indolent summer he went to the pictures
three times a week, with a dreamy appetite
for romantic love and poetry, bored
by adult strictures. In September he entered
his father's office, dumb, without alternative.

His stubborn faith was to be rewarded:
the substance of things hoped for hit him,
love's sweet custard pie, *zoom*,
the town beauty, of doubtful reputation,
bang in the eye, a tall short-sighted girl
to be danced round the Corinthian Ballroom,
alive, laughing, beyond compromise.

2

Together in all weathers we glimpsed them walking
the shadowy docks in the small hours, themselves
a holy presence, the night air spiced
by resinous pine-wood planks, coal
dust, diesel-fumes and cattle-feed. Light
from the iron hulls of small foreign vessels
revealed her lovely face inclined, intent
on his ideas, her long hair shaken out,
and him watching the trees and street lamps
of the Waterside reflected in the Foyle.

Night after night they made merry
hand in hand, kissing in doorways
in the glamorous empty streets of Derry

that echoed their footsteps over the metal bridge
to Violet Street where goodnights were said
while echoes hushed and then again grew clamorous
under his nailed shoes running home to bed.

3

Of all the picture houses that tended
their love, remember St Columb's Hall,
the Catholic flea-pit to which they descended
to see Glen Ford falling for Rita Hayworth
in *Carmen*. They watched the respectable soldier
led astray and astounded by beauty in his arms,
planning love-play as a way of life,
his betrayed duty fraying his nerves and hers,
her protesting body pressed against his knife,
their love, her life-blood leaking away.

4

Her slaves delivered notes across his counter
answering poems with rendezvous
for lunch hours, plotting walks to the bus,
sharing apples and domestic problems.
The late autumn sun slid between leaves
of the plane trees in Shipquay Street,
spangling light on their two brown heads.
Under the great walls of the city they sheltered
waiting for the Rosemount bus
to take him empty away to Eden terrace.
It seemed in nineteen-fifty the gods were merry.

But alas there were legs of clay under his grey
flannels. His ignorance betrayed them.
Any fool should have known to cleave
to a woman like that, to leave well alone;
but he heard himself complaining like Don José
in the film, and all his fierce objections
to society and religion seemed like excuses

when at last she told him, 'Yes, I am yours,
I will go away as long as we don't come back.'

He wasn't ready to say.

5

His finest hour was their final confrontation
outside the Northern Counties Cafeteria
watching her being talked to, wooed away
by the Unionist Association Secretary.

He fell, as if in a fit, and shammed dead,
and she ran to his side, called by a friend,
and knelt and laddered her stockings to take his head
on her lap. He suddenly laughed, all power and joy,
and that was the last straw. She walked away,
a mature woman, contemptuous of play-
acting, ready to rear a family.

He was a free artist, creative, bereft,
lying after she left him, crazy with laughter
still. Her last touch had proved something
forever, and far above the Post Office roof
the stars shone still, all that was left
to aspire to. A marvellous way to go,
painful with clarity and resonance.

'I think you're often better than you know,
a legend in your own time,' said an ex-pupil,
lately, 'and at your own expense.'

The critic, Mrs Longley, was to write
years after,
'He must have had very large
illusions.' By God she was right.

The Egyptian Hotel

I spent my youth as a barman
in the Egyptian Hotel.
My bosses, Antony and Cleopatra,
treated us well.

He was a rich Protestant
with a deprived youth,
she was a sexy Catholic
gypsy who believed in truth.

He was only on holiday
from his virtuous wife,
happy enough, God knows,
but not cut out for the life.

The work ethic rode him.
Embarrassed and sometimes bored
by love, he nagged and she lit off
to their love-nest on the Antrim Road.

She wrote him a last letter,
her head in the gas oven,
'Congratulate your bloody wife;
but remember our loving.'

The Egyptian Hotel, I tell you,
was never the same,
and nor was Antony
after the wife came.

Gentle, she was, forbearing,
and under her employ
we flourished, yet sickened
for the wild spark of joy.

Anthony drank heavy,
the rows were very bitter.
A suitcase on the wardrobe top
enshrined the last letter

and all their love letters
tied in a string.
Man and wife lived out their time,
if you call that living.

The odd thing I remember is
that most of the staff stayed,
and those who left always
left to get married.

The Imperial Theme

Girls were of course strangers
to a man. We explorers
wheedled intimacy, pretended
ingeniously to speak
their language, exchanging
bright cheap beads of fantasy,
words of love, for delectable
cuntland, free trade and grazing
on breast and belly, rest and shelter
in forests of perfumed hair.

We coaxed lust from these
placid animals, preaching
a heady gospel of free love,
bargaining words of tenderness —
these tribes were starving —
then firing parting shots
into the herd, watching them
stir, stampede, rustling off
a few head.

I must admit we worked best
drunk and in darkness.
I never relished the blackened
fire places, slumped figures
weeping in the light of day.

2

The loveliest country
in the New World
was your pale smooth belly
with that tiny pond
southward,
and the slow descent
to sheltered scrubland,
the hidden cave
with its weird formations,
vagina, clitoris, explained
by laws of nature.

Outside, after
the whole climate
was filled with sighs
as we leant smoking
against sheer walls
of white thighs.

At the back of my head
I felt your eyes
following me
all the way down
blessing my journey
crying small cries
of horror
and encouragement.

Rogation Day: Portrush

for Derek Mahon

I stop to consult my diary and think how queer
that in my day farmers can be sincere
kneeling in stiff suits, their rough hands
joined, praying for swaying cornlands,
a big yield, reward for labour, a reply
from the dumb planets and the gaseous sky.

Upstairs my hands grip the shoulders
of a kindly lady. Between the unholy boulders
of her thighs I play Moses with my loins.
Below, when the spinning disc stops, coins
flow in *Sportsland*. Someone has picked the right slot
in the one-armed bandit. I hear the jackpot,

and I ejaculate and the girl-friend sighs.
The farmers stand and rub their eyes
for this is a miracle and all the walls are glass.
They can see through the church and up my ass,
and the boy waging his penny in the one-armed thief.
Lord I am lucky: help thou their unbelief.

A Song of Herself
for Frank Ormsby

One night he followed Romeo,
hoisted himself aloft
up drain-pipes to her balcony.
She told him to piss off.

Wrapped in Romantic attitudes
he didn't know or care.
It took him nearly twenty years
to say, 'Piss off,' to her.

What maybe looked like wiliness
in that girl was fear.
When she gave up her maidenhead
the parents had to hear.

Small comfort to her were her skills.
The ethos that deployed her
won her the boss's son, alas.
The boss's son destroyed her.

Ballad of a Marriage

'This sweet mysterious country
explored by my right hand.
Am I the first, my wife, that's burst
into this silent land?'
She said she hadn't been a whore
but she had lain with men before.

I'd slept with girls myself, but I
was trembling, I was hating
these men, and her, and yet I found
her stories titillating:
first fascination, then disgust;
first pain and then a surge of lust.

Playing with words as children play
with toys had been a thrill;
but now the cuddly lion had jaws,
the little gun could kill.
Freedom and truth, by which I swear,
in fact were more than I could bear.

When she stirred under me I saw
her squirming in delight
in other people's cars and beds,
and sitting up all night,
her face drained white in love's despair
because some man had not been there.

To freeze the pain of this I froze
my love. I read much more
and thought alone and talked to friends
till three a.m. and four.
And came to bed the worse for beer
and was annoyed to have her near.

She cried a lot and fought, surprised;
knowing love she felt the lack.
Love? What was love? I only felt
her dead weight on my back.
We stayed together out of shame
and habit, and the children came.

Younghusband

for Anthony Cronin

1

Lead him, the love discoverer
to a dumb wilderness
where words have made no maps,
the woman's arms his only instructors,
her eyes his campfires.
She is at home here,
a natural savage.
In clean pyjamas
he is a pioneer.

A nation of savage stars
stares at him passing
from the last station
into the darkening hills.

2

There were hard regions of whiteness
she led him through.
The sense of making a journey
he lived up to
with the courage he used to show
in boyish games
adventuring his all
following dog-teams into danger
where nothing to eat would ever grow
where no one was going to build cities.

He shouted, but who knows
what he meant planting
a flag in the dead centre,
the barren summit, naming the place
for his masters, his King.
This was achievement
and there was celebrating,
a breaking out
of last biscuits, a cherished

bottle of champagne
that no one savoured,
then emptiness again.

It is the story of his race.

A polar bear
who lived there
raised his homely head
from a fishing hole
and stared.

3

The Englishman within us all
is true to the wild
solemn ambitions
of a lonely child.

He is one of the English
is he not?
Inspired by Sir Walter Raleigh
and Captain Scott?

He didn't know they were so cruel
and crass.
He liked the sentiment
and sacrifice.

4

Certain phrases
in church services
made the calling of love
his life.
Old maps and metaphors,
moments in novels and plays
expelled him from his back garden,
hungry and argumentative

towards God, Tahiti, The Dark Tower,
ready to set the slughorn to his lips
and blow for true love
or the life of Reilly,
a promised dance
over the hills and far away.

He was born for service;
but the long apprenticeship
sharpened his vision horribly
and exposed his ignorance.

Hairy adventures, dull periods,
pure terror, tenderness,
leafy hollows, nether garments,
bedrooms with curtains drawn at noon
brought him to this bad marriage
the clutches of this harridan
who knows something she can't divulge.

5

'Reach me my tinder box, old crone.
Let us be married and live alone,
wallpaper flats in the city of Leeds,
work for me, woman, condone my misdeeds,
shop for me, feed me, in sunshine and wet,
and night after night we will wrestle and sweat.

Allow me to dream, in my vacant hours,
of gardens I dreamt in before your powers
enthralled me. Indulge my poem-writing,
torment me, teach me the arts of fighting.
Pilgrim, philosopher, poet and saviour
is play to this. It is hard labour

to be intimate, to drink at the source,
to progress at sexual intercourse.

In the jungle of marriage the youth-dream ends
far from the chatter of helpful friends.

6

England, homeland, motherland,
how your beauty stays,
laid brick by brick by history
in the confident old days,

and the legal system, clause by clause,
fought for, binding us yet,
our constitutional government,
our bloody national debt,

the gardens and vicarages,
farms, castles, cottages.
The abbeys and priories
dismantled to build colleges,

the training that grows meaningless
when English leaders imitate
the decadence of foreigners,
monstrous, Italianate.

The home of Empire withers now,
the bee-hive suffers loss,
the hayrick and bright maypole gone,
the clog-dance and the cross.

Tricksters, upstarts, gangsters
have villas on the Downs.
The trickster-gangsters of old days
played lute-songs and wore crowns;

but they won their awful battles!
From that horrific best
the wave comes back heavy
from the old tide of conquest.

7

No smiles, drab indignation:
we take it very hard,
young Cockneys, blacker than your boot,
reciting Avon's bard.

Crassly and ungratefully,
we take it very ill,
Elizabethan splendour
in the streets of Notting Hill,

exuberant West Indians
recalling us to dance,
to warble and take pleasure.
We British look askance,

for courtship is a nervous time,
liberties are taken.
We need new blood pumped in our veins,
not to be forsaken,

the energy of Hong Kong,
Malaya, Pakistan,
Ireland, Australia.
We must take it while we can.

We must sign them up for football,
for the factory, the choir,
and trot our nubile daughters out
to maybe quench their fire.

We are the ineffectual,
the tired-out, the old,
though we have salutary truths
to tell that must be told

of limit and proportion,
of silliness and sin.
It is a complicated world
for lovers to be in.

The First Goodbye Letter

'Dear wife, I don't suppose you understand
my cheerfulness these days with passion cooling,
my love-songs of a bachelor,
my boyish fooling,

the way I lie so easy on my own side
or rise to screw newspaper for the fire?
Crooning over breakfast pans
is all that I desire.

Safely alive in the quiet light of morning,
indulging my fancy alone, acting the clown
is plenty, plenty. I'm reconciled
to letting us all down.

Old girl, don't worry over it, don't argue.
The famous challenge of marriage, when all is said,
is not my scene, the legal arena,
the permanent double bed.

Me? Famous for nothing but giggling, tiptoe,
avoiding parents and other dinosaurs
through fern and aspidistra jungles,
down dangerous corridors?

I'm nowhere, home again, goodbye my honey,
escaping the duns of conscience with ad-lib ruses,
incapable drunk, but always deft
with wry smiles and excuses.'

Mates

I had a few friends in my life.
They've gone, I haven't one.
I notice when you get a wife
friendship is done.

A friend is subtle and funny,
a wife is a bit thick;
but the sort of friends I used to have
had no use for my prick.

Girls have the soft bodies.
Love is a mystic pleasure
that lures you from society,
the male pursuit of leisure.

These dream-boats, these sweet engines
incorporate demands
beyond their little juicy cunts,
their soft breasts and hands.

It's 'Ho' for kitchen equipment
and a more salubrious flat,
a steady job and promotion.
At least it feels like that.

Mr Cordelia

1

In nineteen-sixty, in July
a husband made his young wife cry.
Mr Cordelia, plain and true,
God help the poor bitch marries you,
your truth that lacks the warmth of lies,
the decency to compromise.

Watch him this dull and windy day,
the seventh of their holiday.
There's been a row, he runs away
to sit in Gormley's crass café
and brood and scribble poetry
and watch the fine-etched wavelets pass
beyond geraniums and coarse grass.

Poor kids, they'd been confused and tired
at twenty-two when they had hired
First Derry Church and bought a ring
and made responses promising
some nonsense, at which moment fell
the old ironic citadel
he and his friend had built to cope
with life, to live it without hope.

2

How much that's good a marriage ends,
true solitude and true male friends,
the doing without that made them free.
He only lived for poetry.
So, in a fight, like this today,
his impulse is to walk away
back to his solitude. He strode
off, as from some dull episode.
The job, the children and the wife
were episodes become a life.

And that he's changed just now he sees
among the tasteless buns and teas,
planning to cross the road and buy
a ticket . . . all his energy
shifts from the daydream situation —
creative girls with education
sharing his interests, cottages
where poems would fill the parchment pages.

He thinks only a coward chooses
going back alone, making excuses.
Success must never close her out.
The good life has to be about
a joy accessible to all,
not silly wives going to the wall.
Besides, not only would she wither,
the bitch, she'd take the children with her
into her bitterness. Her will
is dreary but implacable.

He cannot love, he cannot leave;
but he can grieve and make her grieve.

3

Such dull and barren suffering
does not create a better thing.
Old grudges counter new demands
and no one comes with surgeon hands
to cut clean, without fuss or bother,
these two malignant on each other.

Mr Cordelia lost his will
to win and trudged home up the hill.
And, ten years later, still they rage,
untamed birds wilting in a cage
condemned to compromise and doubt
and like to serve the sentence out.

Knock on Your Own Door

It seems right he should knock
on his own door, a stranger
quick to ingratiate, by nature
a bachelor, the wife a landlady
with attractive children.

None of this is conscious
exactly; but watch the mouth
twitch before he turns to face
family. He is seconds late
seeing wife expects kiss,
is dressed special, for birthday
perhaps. This mistake
might expose him; but no,
it passes off in anger — a good ploy.
Resignedly he stumps upstairs
to his study — he does that perfectly —
and yearns at the window, at the skyway
of huge gold clouds and grey.

Now he has boundless energy
pounding amusing letters out
to old friends, or poems,
like coded calls for help:
OH LET ME BE THE MAN
I DREAMED I'D BE.

Silence.

A real contentment holds him
if he is reading, soon
to be called down for the next act.
He kisses children convincingly,
passes plates, eats his tea,
answers questions, sits smoking,
devoutly watches TV.

Who doubts he can keep
this up forever, or till
the audience walks out.

When She's Late Home

When she's late home at night I find I care.
The need in me to love and be loved whines
like a sick beast that can't be made aware
his case is hopeless despite all the signs.

I'll not be easy till he's died.
My livelier beasts are restive and annoyed
to find me so preoccupied.
They scent real futures that could be enjoyed.

They pine; but only I can let them out —
I, cosseting the one I should destroy
that shrinks in hiding from my hearty shout,
that shows no benefit in my employ.

He lost all races he was entered for,
bit harmless guests and piddled on the stair . . .
the beast is love. I'll drop the metaphor.
When she's late home at night I find I care.

Interior Decorating

One night I strode from you to ease my bowels
down collonades of wood. In brass bowls
flames flickered in oil. It was Ancient Greece,
and the mat on the wooden floor was a shaggy fleece
my bare toes savoured. The towel I wore
was a hero's garb. I was running from Helen, my whore
queen, unsatisfied and inexhaustible.
Her tormenting loins will be the ruin of us all.

My dreams were always transforming our bungalow
(it was Alaska, once, with esquimaux),
like sauce or grease-paint covering the true.
Whatever I read was rubbing off on you.
My arms held dark Thai beauties, pale colleens . . .
all sorts beside me where you should have been
if I could have borne you. And Mrs Miniver!
Fled were twenty years since I'd fancied her.

Unhappy marriages are that eccentric,
irrelevant to decent people, sick;
but common. Does anyone hope for a happy ending?
When the couples we know are scathing or condescending,
bored, scared of each other? Reluctantly,
always, they turn towards home, towards bed, towards tea.
Escape we must, or learn to relish the hating,
to dreams, to drink, interior decorating.

Dan the Liberator

Dan danced last night at John McVeagh's
with two attractive wives,
and clearly both of them enjoyed
the evening of their lives;

but people were disturbed,
they were accused, and words of shame
made them and him uncertain, even
sorry that they came.

'Twas Dan himself prepared the tape
the small recorder played:
Bob Dylan, Joni Mitchell, Jo
Venuti — It was great!

Dan loved that house, its drawing rooms,
huge kitchen and huge hall.
Chessmen were moved below, upstairs
the frantic ping-pong ball.

McVeagh's a great competitor,
a wit austerely funny.
His house must be among the most
complete in Ballymoney,

and he, who hates to lose, makes guests
ecstatic when they beat him,
his hard contempt for flashy moves,
his instinct that they cheat him.

Dan drank. He did not like the talk,
not heart-warm, not malicious,
but deadly dull, he thought. Dan then
grew restless and ambitious.

He was a dancer — jiving, waltzing,
High Life, Rock and Roll.
Most husbands won't dance. Dan became
the party's life and soul.

He set up in the kitchen, crying,
'The work-and-mortgage lies
foul up the hall. Come, undertake
life's finest exercise.

'Surely we all admit to being
estranged from deepest joys,
who make our jokes from nagging wives,
vacations, mother-in-laws!

'One can't win. I WILL win,' he yelled,
'On with the dance!' and yet,
if bum and breast grew sweetly conscious
that was the height of it.

He moved out to a small divan
then for a tête-à-tête.
He can't remember what was said,
but he was interested.

His wife observed a husband crying
and with sharp intuition
pumped him for what would prove to be
most useful ammunition.

Like some great bird of prey,
in tones of rich contempt and hate,
she hissed, 'Dan, that girl suffers
a recurrent nervous state.'

'Small wonder, if her husband's crying
at what she's doing with me.
Now you'll cry. Christ, I wish that I
could cry so easily.'

Dan's wife was warming to a theme
for which he'd grown to hate her.
Arrested adolescent's what
she called The Liberator!

He rushed upstairs and won the table-
tennis competition,
and nearly won at chess. Dart-playing
was outside his ambition.

The world was too small for him, singing
Ritorna vincitor
in full voice, as he peed, he broke
the lavatory door,

just turning round. He would replace it
then and there. He'd play
his host chess for a five quid stake . . .
His wife drove him away.

Dan danced last night at John McVeagh's
with two attractive wives,
and clearly both of them enjoyed
the evening of their lives.

He can't recall their names or talk
or by how many sets
he won the ping-pong; but, like Piaf,
he has no regrets.

Late Night Project

The girl behind the counter
is getting on for forty.
She wears a dress so flimsy
we'll simply rip it off her
and say it was a lie.

They've rummaged her so often,
impressing love upon her
will strain our huge resources,
but it's a point of honour,
so drink up and let's try.

The Second Time Around

At last you've gone, as I did before,
slipping out of the front door
to make it with a strange face.
I'm inward torn, haunting
the promenade involuntary
to find you, and yet glad
to return to my room at half-past three
alone. One face of jealousy
is curiosity insatiable, only
to be borne, but bearable: I see
one gradually curbs its energy.

I wish you joy of the common mystery
my theory hoped you'd share,
of which you scorned the possibility:
having the old adventures of youth
over again with more irony and truth
to salt familiar embraces that still
excite us all, like a special line
in popular songs for 'the older person'.

All the accoutrements are there,
in different styles: the underclothes,
for instance, briefer, the fasteners
more various. Sweet nakedness
still seems miraculous.
Lucky for us, the looser skin
on worn bodies grows bright
under the eye of desire
without discreet lighting.

In blemishes may seem
variety, and people presumed
to be living conventional lies
between Cancer Dances and Bingo
are the old crowd in a new disguise,
souls we have known at different stages,
for middle age is not The Middle Ages.

Five American Sonnets

1

At the Thornton's party, after
the reading, after being shy,
after just now starting to sing,
I notice a girl's laughter
and turn to meet blue eyes
in a pretty face. Breath-taking.

In outlandish garb she sits
at my feet, laughing
and listening hard.
The department chairman takes note of it
and says something
sarcastic about visiting bards.

He knows, though envious and older,
beauty rewards the poet and the soldier.

2

Mellissa: a name like that, discovered
in a diary's past day by a jealous
wife would make her see red
then green. Oh, hours of fuss
from sick habits we are bred
to exemplify — more fools us.

With connections my eyes shine!
My late wife's lover's name, whose face
was horribly burned, was Valentine.
Fate has always been strong on farce.
So it is with mellifluous mine —
Mellissa has too large an arse

to be ignored or enjoyed. Ruefully
I must make use of my philosophy.

3

My former wife said I would fuck
my own grandmother, my grandchildren!
Not at all. I searched for hidden
qualities of mind, with no luck.
There was only hunger and pain
in those pretty features. No. Not again!

On a good day the fattest thighs
might be transcended
by glory of the spirit,
but nothing ignited between our eyes.
And there it should have ended
maybe, but I saw merit

in her simple refusal to feel
her disadvantages were real.

4

Next day at our rendezvous
starting cold we got as far
as naked bathing in a Red Indian
clearing. We breast-stroked through
the clear cold river water
and lay together with mundane

emotions. There were no leaves
on the pine-trees above us.
Exposed, good-natured, bored
I listened to stories of her previous loves
that had never come true. Her vocal prose
would never move us toward

intimacies of mind and flesh,
so we covered our nakedness.

5

From the lyric bathing hole
on the Eno river to her European car
parked on the highway,
swinging on branch and bole
of sunlit trees, was not too far,
for happily we did it my way

and really savoured the stopping
on huge flat rocks to gaze
at rapids, like old friends, climbing
down to lave our faces, stepping
together under the blaze
of March sun westwards. Fate's timing

was perfect: my host breezed in
just as our dying fall was wearing thin.

Knocking On

The more I wear glasses
the less well I see.
Mary at the study door
was hazy to me,

hard on eyes to look at,
hard on mind to grasp.
I panicked and slammed on
my spectacles fast

and lost her, rightly,
for glasses are grotesque,
like the ache in my elbows,
the pains in my breast.

Love is for the young ones.
Even if they're not
elegant or gentle
their blood runs hot.

After experience
we measure our resource,
the pulse beats softer
further from the source.

Intricate and careful,
too fond of style,
even the nicest girls
turn away to smile.

Cuchulain at his last post,
Sweeney in the trees,
hands out of plackets
and off plump knees:

I should seek, with those men,
the danger and the wet.
Pull back the sheet, love,
soon, but not yet.

Autumn in Portrush: 1974

Tonight is raining beautifully,
Kerr Street is glossy black. The lights
on the coast road across the bay
are strung out small and bright
above the cliffs, reflecting blurrily
in the cold restless sea.

Here I live, and I'm here at three
in the morning inspecting the streets,
windy, echoing, empty.
Lately I find it hard to sleep
so I work late and walk alone,
hard-pressed and excited at forty-one.

Joyce, for his hell-fire preacher, writes
that sex is a 'tingling of the nerves'. Odd
to be risking Hell for that. But all delight is
a tingling of nerves, the Peace of God
as much as the glow a hot toddy
of Bush spreads through your body.

I drove my Vauxhall into the bright
oasis of a filling station. 'They got
Tommy Herron. They found his body tonight,'
the attendant mouthed, wanting what I could not
give him, a brother's answer. 'Dead?'
'Aye, they shot him through the head.'

Today before lunch was the loveliest
in my life, why, I can't say. Boisterous
wind, warm September, my mind at rest
but energetic, rereading Joyce,
so much the greatest of us all
and yet so sick and small.

Molly says YES; but James lacked the gift
of poetry, for taking the nerves seriously,
for all his ingenious attempts to sift
all of reality exhaustively,
he was mimicking other voices.
Only a self rejoices.

I read books, out walking, lifting my eyes
to say, 'Hello, Declan,' to the Rohdich boy.
People watch my behaviour with surprise
to my surprise. Some seem to enjoy
having a writer in their town;
but others would put me down.

My boss took me aside to show
anonymous poison-pen letters
from nutty locals claiming to know
dirty secrets of their lonely betters.
'Drugs and orgies?' No, all I can use
is old-fashioned: wife and kids and the muse.

Alone

His body and hers are touching
because they have no spare bed
and can't afford an hotel.
To get into this state
took twenty years of give and take,
delight and learning, nervousness,
new challenges, changes, distrust,
despair, conciliation, up and down,
year after year.

Strained, waiting for sleep
they seem to hear a fast jet
whispering light years away
cutting a white furrow
in the moonlit sky, loaded
with travellers, rich enough
and free, warmed by whisky,
joking about tomorrow.

The Son Defends His Father

'Some men are the play-actors
of their own ideal.'

Nietzsche

Said the mother, 'Be good to your wife child,
not like your selfish father was to me.
That bugger had no sense of family.'
Her son held his fiancée's hand and smiled,

'Ah, don't complain about daddy. All the lives
he infringed on and girls he befriended
I think to him were a sort of extended
family. They were all his wives.'

Divorce

The woman became an imperial power
and we got rid of her;
but how am I better off,
and how are the childer?

Every day I pause frustrated,
nagging like she used to.
Is this what it is to be
a free republic? I bluster

whine and moralise, self-pityingly
like she did. No, not quite.
I'm only saying it's hard work
to live, to govern right.

The Work of the Penis

1

The day of the wedding
was blessed by good weather.
Is it holy, these families
coming together?

Is this money well spent?
Is there joy in this meeting?
With the pick of the natural
wild world for eating,

is ham, chicken salad
with Heinz salad cream
and soup, sweet and coffee
the Irish bride's dream?

2

We are drunk, throw the bouquet.
Farewells fade away,
and two travel westward
through the hot day.

The wog in the woodpile,
the ghost at the feast,
is bulging his trousers,
the dirty wee beast,

and the work of the penis
will, brutal and hot,
exalt their two bodies
or it will not.

3

When, rampant and couchant,
together they lie,
may the lark in the clear air
be lost in the sky,

in the lull of their struggle
when two winners yield,
moist forehead to forehead,
a stook in a field.

May the rubbing of muscles,
the breaking of bread,
be humble and holy
in church and in bed.

May all the world's lovers,
all husbands and wives,
get lost in forever
for once in their lives.

Birth

I don't remember it too well
but I hear tell
there's great times inside the womb —
even in Ulster.
In there's the original snug,
the landlady's your friend,
quiet nights all day
inside, out of the wind,
tucking it away.

But good things come to an end.
The powers that be
enforce closing time
harshly. After a hard struggle
you're out in the street
dry, suffering sunlight.

Ah, poor wain, upside down,
squeezed out. A giant has you
by the ankles and slaps your bum.
The heart that beat so quiet
shows he's boss, a slave-driver,
a dynamo: for him the lungs swell,
the mouth gapes involuntary
and raw air pours in. Hunger
is coming. For wailing, for sucking,
the wain discovers a mouth on him.

Wiped clean, they call it:
the bruised defenceless babe
is wrapped in kindly substitutes,
and that's it from now on.

Exiled forever from gently
rocking waters, sea creature
ashore, the cord severed,
the gates forever closed.

Wherever the child's off to
is the long way home,
with no sense of direction.

Like exiles we roam.

My Friend the Instrument

She sits on the chair opposite,
my much-loved guitar.
On her, sweet-toned and true, I know
what everything is for:

the corset waist, the flat shining
belly. My fingers dance
over her dark well on strings.
I feel her resonance.

Brass frets divide her rosewood neck.
Engines for tightening,
tiny, of brass, inexorably
hold each graded string,

strings that stretch down her body
each to its ivory peg.
The silly bitch stands on her head
crying, 'Look, no arms, one leg!'

I settle her across my thighs
to strum her and transport
her and our audience. We can
make music of a sort.

Like lovers, I'm too good for her
and she's too good for me,
neither can search the other's full
potentiality.

And that's the way it goes,
we both make music as we can,
me, made incompetently by God,
she, competently by man.

Qualified Lovers

1

Degrees are just bits of paper.
But the paper's indicative:
you have to be clever
to pass exams in whatever,
add, analyse, live.

Before we embrace, my darling,
here where the nightingales sing,
before we get down to essentials
can you show me credentials,
A-levels, anything?

2

The Beat hero of yesterday,
Jack Kerouac,
who, we had no doubt,
was letting it all hang out,
was really holding it all back.

Marie C. Stopes,
far from being superhuman
sensual and free
was actually
an impossible woman.

She made up her own rules
and still was unhappy;
but that doesn't prove
she couldn't love,
she might have been just unlucky.

3

'Leave me be and I'm happy'
is OK for the talented.
There are not many such,
the ungainly need a crutch,
or so Auden said.

To have common sense is the thing
and still be radical,
to enjoy square meals
while exploring ideals
and accepting the inevitable.

Impotence

1

There were nights he would bend to me
and whisper,
'The wee bird sings no more,'
not vulgar,
objectively,
speaking in metaphor.

Solid as the old steam
engines he once
drove, and stout
and stately, he ordered
Guinness and whisky
that I poured out

and carried to him,
to his shrine
in the dark bar
where he waited,
benign, smiling,
an Ulster Buddha,

He was well turned out
always. His plain clothes
were impeccable;
but words failed him,
he sat like the frog in the story
at the bottom of a well.

I add these verses
for my mother
who urged me to say
how David,
an old-age pensioner,
paid his way

in the prosperous company
of George the grocer
and my humorous father,
how they teased him,
and how David
was a better man than either.

2

If, years later,
the grown waiter's luck
is such
that beautiful women
like ripe fruit
at the first touch

come away in his hand,
alas, potency
is no longer there,
and the lack in his loins
is reproach almost
too poignant to bear.

He knows,
artful and tender,
that love is a game.
He believes when girls say,
'It doesn't matter, darling.'

But all the same.

3

It's style we remember
people for,
and the crack:
Cleopatra and Antony
and David Mackeral
with the wall at his back.

A great character!
Barflies felt privileged
to stop at his table
and hear his few words,
profoundly slow
and memorable.

And yet,
when Dionysius touched him,
he tried to sing . . .
erect, wordless,
tuneless,
self conducting,

and the drunk youngsters
intuited *Black
Velvet Band*
or whatever,
applauding,
reaching for his hand.

David seemed to be waiting
for the point
of a difficult joke,
innocent, expressionless,
and then
his smile broke!

Dear old friend,
with all your limitations,
to sing!
Your wee bird could
no more,
and mine is faltering,
was always faltering.

Lily

He sets aside a lunch hour
to write a valediction for his wife,
Lily, whose virtues fostered life.
Groping in the desk drawer
for matches his hands find
tablets she'd bought for him to counteract
some vitamin deficiency. Now that
was intelligent and kind!
So why now the obscene gesturing,
the vindictive exploiting of wains
to get her way? Are these the birth pains
of a new Lily, or Lily festering?

Olive and Davy

When conversation failed
the family album came down.
A portrait of Auntie Olive
in her BA gown

stunned me, hair sculpted
neatly round her ears,
so beautiful I stole it
and had it for years.

When age and her last illness
ravaged her face
the gold hair still shone
with all its old grace.

I remembered it last night
when Uncle Davy died.
Was that why he wanted
no one at his side

this last year, a widower?
We knew he'd seen more
of the wide world than most of us,
Australia, Samoa,

Nigeria; but not much,
we presumed, of life,
him with his speech defect
and his lovely wife.

Uncle Davy, very quiet,
and Olive, my Aunt
so strikingly beautiful,
so gay and so fluent

his one rebuke in public
echoed like a riot,
telling his lovely back-seat driver,
'Olive, be quiet.'

The winter she died
he brought sweets and sherry
to my mother's bridge evenings
and got mildly merry.

We hardly broached his bottle;
but always next time
he brought the same parcel,
courteous and kind.

Suddenly he grew, it seemed,
impatient for death,
and symptoms followed, pallor,
shortness of breath,

a new, old man, Davy,
blank, impolite,
preferring no company
night after night

to neighbourly solicitude,
an idle rout
trying to perk him up,
eking him out.

He died. This is an old story
from the common stock:
an old crock longing
for another old crock,

longing on beyond youth,
beyond beauty's decay,
beyond the grave — so it seems—
for Olive, Davy.